The Skinny on Networking

the skinny on™

networking

maximizing the power of numbers

Jim Randel

ISBN: 978-0-9844418-1-5
Ebook ISBN: 978-0-9844418-2-2
Library of Congress: 2010905713

Illustration/Design: Lindy Nass
Rebecca Kunzmann

For information address Rand Media Co, 265 Post Road West, Westport, CT, 06880 or call (203) 226-8727.

The Skinny On™ books are available for special promotions and premiums. For details contact: Donna Hardy, call (203) 226-8727 or visit our website: www.theskinnyon.com

Printed in the United States of America

10 9 8 7 6 5 4 3 2
9 2 5 – 4 9 1 9

the skinny on™

Welcome to a new series of publications entitled **The Skinny On™,** a progression of drawings, dialogue and text intended to convey information in a concise and entertaining fashion.

In our time-starved and information-overloaded culture, most of us have far too little time to read. As a result, our understanding of important subjects often tends to float on the surface – without the insights of thinkers and teachers who have spent years studying these subjects.

Our series is intended to address this situation. Our team of readers and researchers has done a ton of homework preparing our books for you. We read everything we could find on the topic at hand and spoke with the experts. Then we mixed in our own experiences and distilled what we have learned into this "skinny" book for your benefit.

Our goal is to do the reading for you, identify what is important, distill the key points, and present them in a book that is both instructive and enjoyable to read.

Although minimalist in design, we do take our message very seriously. Please do not confuse format with content. The time you invest reading this book will be paid back to you many, many times over.

INTRODUCTION

You've probably heard the expression "It's not what you know, it's who you know."

Well, there's a lot of truth to it.

Of course you always need to work hard at your endeavor of choice ("what you know"). Your value in the business world depends on what you can do for people. Therefore, you must have a skill, information or expertise that others will consume – that people will pay for.

BUT, having that skill, information or expertise is often not enough to maximize your potential.

You need people – a network to help you distribute your skills. You need people to help you find a job, a loan, customers, or the right partner.

This book is about creating and maintaining your network. I hope you will give us the hour or so it will take to read this book. I assure you that it will be one of the best hours you have ever spent.

"The ability to achieve our goals, fulfill our missions, and make our contributions to the world depends as much on our social capital (the resources available in and through personal and business networks) as it does on our human capital (knowledge, expertise, and experience). People who build the right networks get the resources they need when they need them."

Achieving Success Through Social Capital,
Wayne Baker (Josey-Bass, 2000)

Hi, I'm Jim Randel, founder of The Skinny On book series.

1

Today we are going to take a swing at a hugely important topic – networking.

Networking means different things to different people so let's start with a definition.

2

"NETWORKING" IS DEVELOPING AND UTILIZING RELATIONSHIPS WITH OTHER PEOPLE.

I realize that this definition is broad.

So, I've made a list for you with specific activities that fall within the ambit of networking.

MY LIST

1. Staying in touch with people you've already met.

2. Meeting new people.

3. Doing research to find the person(s) who can assist you.

4. Using online resources to identify someone you know who knows someone you want to meet.

5. Increasing social capital.

6. Entertaining and helping others – creating a desire for reciprocity.

7. Building positive word of mouth.

8. Marketing your expertise.

9. Joining groups that foster natural connections.

10. Asking for introductions and referrals.

My list is not meant to be all-inclusive. Going from the broad to the specific and now back to the broad, networking is **any activity** that helps you develop relationships with others.

The good news is that like golf, you can always get better at networking. There are strategies and techniques to learn. We are going to discuss the most important of these.

I'm now going to introduce you to Billy and Beth, the heroes of our story.

They are both good at what they do. **But**, neither of them is a very good networker – and so neither is in a position to maximize his or her potential.

Meet Billy. He's 28 years old. He teaches history at the local high school. But his love is music, and his dream is to teach music at the college level.

Meet Beth, Billy's wife. She's 26 and an attorney. She works for a law firm in New York City. Beth loves the practice of law. Her aspiration is to become a partner and that means bringing in clients.

This evening I'm going to give Billy a call and introduce myself to him. And later in our story, I'll try to help Beth.

BILLY AND BETH HAVING DINNER

"Beth, I'm starting to hit the wall in the classroom. I really care about the kids, but I'm constantly thinking about Mozart while explaining the Civil War."

"Maybe it's time for a change, Billy."

"I agree, Beth, but we need the money from my teaching. I can't just up and quit."

"Aren't there openings for music teachers at the college level?"

13

14

"Kind of a weird coincidence …
are you going to call him back?"

"I'm not sure."

Billy does get around to
calling me.

But, first I want to make a
point:

As you heard, Billy was
suspicious when I called.
That's the first reaction
most people have when
approached by **someone
they don't know.**

Human nature forces us to act cautiously when someone we don't know advances toward us. Even if that person has good intentions, it's hard for us to discern motive and so our reflex is to pull back.

And, that's exactly why networking is so important!!

NETWORKING LOWERS INTERPERSONAL BARRIERS.

Once you've met someone, you've created a mini-bond. You can now approach that person without triggering the caution people usually feel toward someone they don't know.

Similarly, if you are introduced or referred to a person by someone he or she knows, you are not a stranger. He is expecting your advance. He feels OK about it because he's been prepared by someone familiar to him.

A major objective of networking is to dilute the wariness people feel when approached or contacted by a stranger.

You do that by putting yourself in positions to meet people – preferably in comfortable situations. You also do that by asking for introductions from someone who knows the person you want to meet.

And finally, you can lower the uncertainty people feel toward strangers by marketing yourself in ways that establish your credibility before you introduce yourself.

But, before we get into connecting with strangers, let's talk about people **you already do know** – acquaintances, friends and family.

NETWORKING IS ABOUT ACCESSING PEOPLE WHO CAN HELP YOU.

EVERYONE YOU HAVE EVER MET CAN POTENTIALLY HELP YOU.

This is my high-school yearbook. I have lost touch with almost everyone in the book. Ditto for my college and law school classes.

Shame on me.

Among the mistakes I have made in my life, I would put at the very top the number of people I have lost touch with. This error has cost me both personally and professionally.

If you are in high school or college, it may be hard for you to envision your classmates as future movers and shakers. But some may be. And some of them may be in positions to help you.

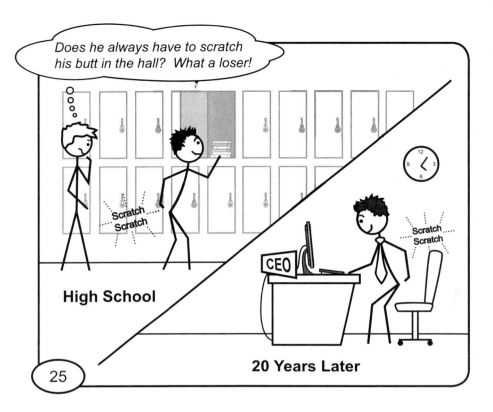

25

Social media sites like Facebook have made staying in touch easier than ever. But don't stop there. Reach out to people by phone or e-mail. Get together if appropriate.

26

If you went to high school with any of the people below, you should have stayed in touch.

Want to guess who they are?

A

B

C

D

E

A. Bill Gates.

B. Sarah Palin

C. Ben Bernacke – Chairman of the Federal Reserve.

D. Hillary Clinton ... no, of course, Oprah Winfrey!

E. That's me.

YOU NEVER KNOW WHO MAY ONE DAY BE IN A POSITION TO HELP YOU ACHIEVE YOUR GOALS.

DON'T LOSE TOUCH.

OK, time to get back to our story. I have a feeling that Billy is about to give me a call.

"Hi, Billy, I'm glad you called me. No, I'm not trying to sell you something. I'm just interested in giving you my thoughts about networking. Some ideas that may help you get a job teaching music at the college level."

31

ONE WEEK LATER

"Billy, if you have the ability, I may be able to help you find a position teaching music at the college level."

"That's great … are you in the music world?"

32

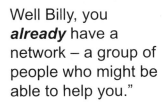

Well Billy, you **already** have a network – a group of people who might be able to help you."

"I wish that were true but I don't think so. If I knew someone hiring college music teachers, I would be teaching college music already."

35

"Excuse me, Billy, I have to go to the restroom."

I don't really have to go to the restroom … I just want to get away from Billy to tell you about a book I just read, Bob Beaudine's **The Power of Who**.

MEN

36

Beaudine's book is about networking. He believes the best approach is to start by contacting people you already know.

Well this is a little awkward.

"You already know someone right now who knows the person who will help you achieve your goal or hire you or introduce you to the person you need to meet."

The Power of Who
Bob Beaudine (Hachette, 2009)

Beaudine proposes that you make a list of 100 people he calls your **WHO**. These are people you know and who will be the most willing to help you.

Then you make a list of 40 people he calls your **WHAT**. These are people in positions to hire or otherwise give you what you want.

Mr. Beaudine's premise is that successful networking means identifying and asking your **WHO** to help you meet your **WHAT**.

I'm going to introduce Billy to Bob Beaudine's thinking about WHO's and WHAT's. But, let's have a little fun with him first.

If you have never seen Abbott & Costello's hilarious comedy sketch, **_Who's on First?_**, please go to YouTube and watch it as soon as possible.

**Abbott and Costello's
"Who's On First?"**

BACK AT THE TABLE

"Billy, I recently read a book
that recommends you speak
to your **WHO**."

"OK, so
who?"

Sorry, I couldn't help myself.

Bob Beaudine does have a serious point however: when you have a specific need, you should start your networking by informing your friends and family what you're seeking to achieve.

Some people neglect to do that because they presume they already know what their friends and family can do for them. That's a mistake.

Studies have shown that even among very close relationships (like marriages) there are gaps in what one knows about the other.

Do not assume you already know what your friends and family can do for you!

> *"Most people operate with inaccurate and incomplete mental maps ... As a result, they don't see or tap into the resources available (to them) through their networks, and are thus much less successful than they could be."*
>
> *Achieving Success Through Social Capital*,
> Wayne Baker (Josey-Bass, 2000)

WHEN REACHING OUT FOR ASSISTANCE START WITH YOUR INNER CIRCLE.

DON'T ASSUME YOU ALREADY KNOW WHAT THEY CAN OR CAN'T DO FOR YOU … OR, WHO THEY KNOW.

Here's one suggestion for reaching out to people you already know.

Go to your e-mail program and type in the letter "A." Then scroll down as it displays everyone you've corresponded with whose address begins with an "A." Then ditto for "B" and so on.

You can then select the people you want to send an e-mail to – announcing your objective. Here's what Billy might write to his e-mail contacts:

> **Hi ... it's Billy.**
>
> **U may not know this about me but I've always wanted to teach music at the college level.**
>
> **Do u know anyone who does that?**
>
> **Do u know anyone in college administration?**
>
> **Pls help with leads and/or ideas.**
>
> **Thx.**

You can, of course, send that message to everyone in your e-mail directory. The problem is you might send it to the wrong person.

For example, Billy might not want the principal of the high school where he teaches to see that e-mail. Or, the parent of a student who e-mailed him recently. Therefore I suggest taking your time and identifying just those individuals you want to receive your e-mail.

Note that the e-mail I suggested Billy write **was specific** as to what he wants to do and what he's asking the recipient to do.

When reaching into your network for assistance, you must tell people **exactly** what you want them to do.

Recently I got a call from a friend asking my help getting his recently-graduated son a job. Please tell me how I am supposed to respond to this:

"Hi Jim. I know you have an extensive network and I was wondering if you could help Ralph get a job. ... Well, he's not sure what he wants to do. He majored in economics in college... solid A average. Good with people. Wants something fun and exciting – oh yes, challenging as well. He's one of those young people who loves to be challenged!!"

No matter how motivated I am to help my friend and his son, he gave me nothing specific to work with.

As Tom Cruise said to his football-player client in the movie, *Jerry McGuire*:

"Help me help you."

GREAT NETWORKERS USE ALL AVAILABLE TOOLS.

Billy used e-mail in reaching out to friends and family. There are many other digital tools.

The internet is the greatest boon to networking ever.

There are many ways the internet can help you network. Here are five:

1. Creating and maintaining a database.
2. Uncovering commonalities. Let me elaborate.

The internet can help you discover people with whom you have something in common.

Let's say, for example, you want to find out whether you're connected to anyone who works at Apple. There are sites that can help you. These sites search the Apple employee base and then match it with your contacts, and contacts of contacts, to see if you have a link to anyone.

These sites can also identify people at Apple who went to the same school as you did or, belong to similar organizations as you do.

Contacting Apple is much easier if you have an entrée.

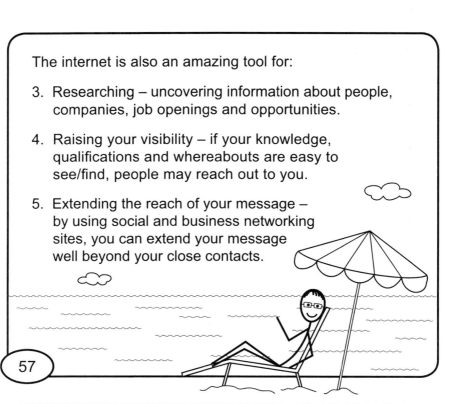

The internet is also an amazing tool for:

3. Researching – uncovering information about people, companies, job openings and opportunities.

4. Raising your visibility – if your knowledge, qualifications and whereabouts are easy to see/find, people may reach out to you.

5. Extending the reach of your message – by using social and business networking sites, you can extend your message well beyond your close contacts.

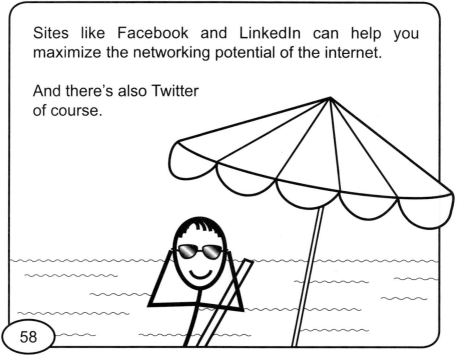

Sites like Facebook and LinkedIn can help you maximize the networking potential of the internet.

And there's also Twitter of course.

Tweets – very short messages – are one way to get the attention of people who have agreed to receive your updates. These people are your followers.

And because tweets are so easy to retweet, or forward to others, Twitter can be a great tool for communicating what you need or want to accomplish.

BuffBilly made a decision! going to make a job change. want to teach music at college level. pls RT!
4 hours ago

The internet supercharges your networking activities because it allows you to identify and connect with people you may not know well (or at all).

When your networking is limited to people who know you well, you're not maximizing the potential of what networking can do for you.

Great networkers learn that sometimes the best resources for information and assistance are people they are not even that close to.

LET'S SEE HOW BILLY DID WITH HIS E-MAIL TO FRIENDS AND FAMILY.

"Any luck with your job search?"

"Not much, Jim. None of my friends or family knows anyone who can help me. I'm actually more discouraged than before I started."

63

**NETWORKING IS
HARD WORK.**

THINK: NET-<u>WORK</u>.

64

"Billy, networking is not a one-shot deal. You don't send out one e-mail to friends and family and then give up if nothing happens.

Now you must expand the circle of who you reach out to – acquaintances and others you may not know well. In fact, I want to tell you about the principle of weak ties."

"Weak ties??"

THE PRINCIPLE OF WEAK TIES STATES THAT SOMETIMES YOUR MOST PRODUCTIVE NETWORKING WILL BE WITH PEOPLE YOU ARE NOT THAT CLOSE TO.

"A weak tie is the relationship you have with a person who knows you – but not well, who you don't see often and who you don't have a strong bond with. You might think of these people as acquaintances.

What's important to understand is that these people are often the ones who can illuminate the path from where you are to where you want to be."

A VERY INTERESTING STUDY

In 1974 a man named Mark Granovetter did an extensive study of how people found jobs. Even though this study preceded the internet (can you imagine a world without Craigs List?), his findings are still relevant today.

Granovetter's research revealed that of those people who learned of a job through a personal contact, the great majority got their lead from someone they were not close to – usually just an acquaintance.

"Acquaintances, as compared to close friends, are more prone to move in different circles than one's self. Those to whom one is closest are likely to have the greatest overlap in contact with those one already knows, so that the information to which they are privy is likely to be much the same as that which one already has."

Getting A Job: A Study of Contacts and Careers
Mark Granovetter (Univ. of Chicago Press, 1975)

69

The principle of weak ties works because acquaintances often travel in different circles than do you, your friends, and your family.

If you can motivate your acquaintances to help you, you expand your horizons as you are now networked to a whole new crowd of people.

70

IT'S TIME TO LEARN ABOUT A VERY
IMPORTANT CATEGORY OF PEOPLE:

CONNECTORS

It might seem an odd transition but I'd now like to talk to you about Paul Revere. Don't worry, eventually this will all make sense.

Paul Revere, as you probably know, is famous for a horse ride he took on April 18, 1775. An American colonist, Revere's role was to warn his neighbors that the British were amassing in Boston for an invasion into the Massachusetts countryside.

And, Revere was very effective. By the time the British reached the town of Lexington, they were met with an organized colonial militia.

Paul Revere was not the only rider out that night in April warning local militia about the British. While Revere rode north, a man named William Dawes rode south.

But, the colonists did not respond to Dawes' warning.

Why? What was the difference between the two men? Was it just that Revere had a louder voice?

Well, not actually, but **metaphorically, yes!!!**

73

Paul Revere was what Malcolm Gladwell termed a "connector" in his great book, **The Tipping Point**.

Revere was outgoing. He was a joiner, a member of several organizations and clubs. He pursued many different activities – each with a separate circle of acquaintances.

Dawes, on the other hand, was a solitary man. He was not nearly as well known as Revere. And when it was time to warn the colonists, his words did not carry nearly the same weight as did Revere's.

74

"Paul Revere was ... a Connector. He was, for example, gregarious and intensely social. ... He was a fisherman and a hunter, a cardplayer and a theater-lover, a frequenter of pubs and a successful businessman. He was active in the local Masonic Lodge and was a member of several select social clubs. He was ... a man blessed with an 'uncanny genius for being at the center of events.'"

The Tipping Point, Malcolm Gladwell
(Little Brown, 2000)

75

GOOD NETWORKING MAY REQUIRE FINDING A CONNECTOR – AND SOLICITING HIS OR HER HELP.

76

As an example, Billy might try to find a connector in the academic world – someone who is active in a lot of different organizations, and who has his or her ear to the ground. Such an individual might produce some good leads for Billy.

The genius of connectors is **the diversity** of the people they know and associate with.

As we have discussed, when you limit your networking to friends and family, you minimize your reach as you often double back on the same people. That's why effective networking often requires reaching out to acquaintances ("weak ties").

A connector understands that. The connector extends himself or herself to **a broad range** of people – working his or her way into many **different camps**.

LET'S TALK ABOUT KEVIN BACON

Perhaps you remember when people were saying that everyone in the entertainment world was connected to Kevin Bacon by just six steps – the whole "six degrees of separation" thing.

Let me tell you the history of that thinking, and the facts behind it.

SIX DEGREES OF SEPARATION

In the 1960's a man named Stanley Milgram did a study. He asked 200 people in Nebraska (Point A) to get a letter (snail mail) to a man in Massachusetts (Point B) none of them knew. Each person at Point A had to send the letter to someone he knew, hoping that person would then know someone who might know someone who would know the man in Massachusetts (Point B).

Milgram wanted to know how many steps it would take to get the letter from Point A to Point B.

On average, it took six steps. In other words, six people had to forward the letter before it got to the individual in Massachusetts.

THE TRUTH BEHIND
SIX DEGREES OF SEPARATION

From Milgram's study came the idea that everyone on earth is connected to everyone else on earth by only six steps. But, there isn't one piece of evidence in support of this theory. In fact, many people think that the whole idea is ridiculous:

"You've heard that there are 'six degrees of separation' between you and anybody else on earth that you would like to meet. ... Ain't true. Sorry, we hate to burst your bubble on such a lovely idea, but it's one of those urban myths ...."

The 29% Solution,
Ivan Misner (Greenleaf, 2008)

SO IS THE WHOLE KEVIN BACON THING JUST SILLY?

Actually, NO. It turns out that Kevin Bacon is a connector.

In fact, people (computers) have studied and measured Bacon's connectivity.

In the analysis Kevin is given the number 0 as the center of his own universe. Any actor or actress who has worked on a film with Kevin is given the number 1. Then, any actor or actress who has worked on a film with someone who has worked on a film with Kevin is given the number 2. And so on.

About 360,000 actors and actresses were given a number. The average rating (how close someone is to Kevin) was 2.86.

That means **lots** of actors and actresses are less than 3 steps away from Kevin. In other words, if you wanted an introduction to your favorite actor or actress, Kevin would be a good place to start.

Why is Kevin so well connected?

Well, Kevin is a very versatile actor. He has starred in light-hearted romps like *Footloose* and *Animal House* and in serious films like *Diner* and *A Few Good Men*. This diversity explains Kevin's connectivity.

Each of us can try to emulate Kevin Bacon and other connectors by expanding the breadth and scope of people we reach out to or, are open to. Often this requires moving out of our comfort zone.

We all gravitate to people whose interests and philosophies are similar to ours. But, that's not always the best path to networking excellence. Connecting with dissimilar folks can be both personally and professionally fulfilling.

That is what connectors do.

LEAVING YOUR COMFORT ZONE

"Discomfort is good. Most people interpret discomfort as a warning sign telling them to avoid something. The opposite is true for networking. Discomfort is a sign that you're doing something right. If you're not feeling uncomfortable, then you aren't moving out of your comfort zone. For example, meeting someone who is just like you is more comfortable than meeting someone who is different from you, but meeting dissimilar people diversifies networks."

Achieving Success Through Social Capital,
Wayne Baker (Josey-Bass, 2000)

"The road to comfort is crowded and it rarely gets you there. Ironically, it's those who seek out discomfort that are able to make a difference and find their footing."

Linchpin, Seth Godin
(Penguin, 2010)

Great connectors are instinctively good at reaching out to all types of people.

If you don't have the time or interest to become a connector, you might instead identify the connectors in your world … and try to connect with them.

In Keith Ferrazzi's book on networking, **Never Eat Alone**, he devotes an entire chapter to "Connecting with Connectors." His strategy is to figure out who are the connectors in his world and develop a relationship with them.

Today Ferrazzi knows a lot of connectors. If he woke up one morning and decided he wanted to be a college music teacher, he would reach out to his connectors.

And presumably one of them would know someone who knew someone who knew someone, and before you could say "Paul Revere" three times quickly, Ferrazzi would be interviewing for an opening to teach music at some university.

Keith Ferrazzi

This is an appropriate juncture to tell you about one of the most amazing connectors I've ever met ... a man named Steve Siegel.

Steve Siegel is a commercial real estate broker in New York City – the toughest real estate arena in the world.

Steve Siegel is consistently one of the top performers in the business – earning millions of dollars in commissions every year. In fact, in 2009 Steve was the #1 broker in the CB Richard Ellis company – 12,000 brokers worldwide, all good at what they do.

Steve is a natural people person. He reaches out to people of all social, economic and cultural strata. He has no particular comfort zones. He is comfortable with and curious about everyone.

About 15 years ago I was at a cocktail party and Steve extended his hand to introduce himself.

"Hi, I'm Steve Siegel."

"I'm Jim Randel. I've heard your name before. I've heard you're a very successful real estate broker."

"I've been fortunate, Jim, but **tell me about yourself**."

I like this guy.

A GREAT WAY TO BUILD YOUR NETWORK IS TO ASK EVERY PERSON YOU MEET TO TELL YOU ABOUT HIM OR HERSELF.

And Steve goes on to ask me lots of questions about my law and real estate businesses.

His interest felt genuine and his eyes never flitted around the room while we were talking.

After about ten minutes he excused himself, explaining he needed to say "hello" to our host.

BUT THE STORY DOES NOT END THERE ...

Six months later, I get a call from Steve.

"Jim, how have you been?

Haven't seen you since the cocktail party. How did that deal you were working on in Milford ever turn out?"

Notice that Steve began the conversation by asking about a deal I had mentioned to him when we met six months earlier.

That was important.

It showed me he had been listening to me.

It re-established him as a genuine guy, interested in matters that were important to me. Immediately the six-month gap between our having talked was bridged.

SUGGESTION: WITHIN 24 HOURS OF MEETING SOMEONE FOR THE FIRST TIME, MAKE NOTES OF HOW YOU MET HER, WHAT SHE DOES, WHAT YOU LEARNED ABOUT HER INTERESTS, FAMILY, ETC.

Steve then goes on to tell me he heard through the grapevine that a large company in New York City was interested in moving its headquarters.

He found out that the CEO of this company, a man named Eric, lived in Westport, Connecticut. He asked whether I knew him.

"Steve, I actually met him for about 30 seconds a few months ago. He was leaving a party as I was entering. But I did introduce myself, and I think he would remember me."

"Well, if he were willing to hire me to help his company relocate, it would be great for me, and since you are a broker, I can pay you a referral fee."

So I decide to try to contact Eric. His home phone number was listed and I called him.

"Hi, Eric. This is Jim Randel. I met you very briefly a few months ago at Mary Jones' house. You were leaving as I was walking in and we introduced ourselves.

Eric, this is a business call, so if you prefer, I can call you at your office."

101

"No, that's OK. I remember our meeting. Tell me what you're calling about."

"A buddy of mine is a top real estate broker in New York City. He heard your company was considering a move. He asked me to introduce him to you.

If you are open to it, I would like to arrange a get-together for the three of us in the City."

102

And Eric suggests that I call his assistant and set up an appointment.

Now, of course, it does not always work quite this well. He could have easily turned me away but perhaps because we had met face to face … or, because we had a mutual acquaintance in Mary Jones … or because I was quick and to the point, he agreed to the meeting.

EVEN IF YOU'VE MET SOMEONE FOR THIRTY SECONDS, YOU HAVE AN OPENING FOR CONTACTING HIM OR HER.

A MONTH LATER, WE HAVE A ONE-HOUR BREAKFAST. ERIC ASKS A LOT OF QUESTIONS BUT WAS NON-COMMITTAL.

STEVE AND ERIC EXCHANGED E-MAIL ADDRESSES AND WE ALL LEFT.

105

FOUR MONTHS LATER, I GET A CALL FROM STEVE

"Hello. … Hey Steve … how have you been? We haven't talked since breakfast with Eric … Did you ever get the assignment?"

"Jim, we not only got the assignment, we just yesterday consummated a lease agreement to move Eric's company into new space. It's a sizeable deal.

Do you want to know what your referral fee is?"

106

I had no idea what Steve meant by a "sizeable deal." I'm thinking a $25,000 referral fee would be nice.

"Of course."

"How does $750,000 sound?"

As it turned out, Eric's company's move was one of the largest deals in New York City that year. The commission was $5 million and my share was $750,000!

Obviously this type of deal is once in a lifetime. But, it emphasized for me the importance of a broad network. Even if I was the cleverest real estate broker in America, without having met Steve and reaching out to Eric, I could never have earned that kind of return on my time ($750,000 per hour).

Of course, Steve didn't do badly either. By networking with me, he created a bridge to Eric, and from there he pocketed a several million dollar commission.

KNOWING THE RIGHT PEOPLE CAN BE VERY LUCRATIVE.

"I have made my living reaching out to people. Along the way I have made a lot of friends … and a little bit of money, too."

Steve Siegel

By reaching out to people you not only create business opportunities, you also open yourself to new life experiences. And you may make great friends along the way.

Both Steve and Eric are now close friends of mine.

NETWORKING IS NOT JUST ABOUT BUSINESS. NETWORKING IS ABOUT INCREASING YOUR DEPTH AND BREADTH AS A PERSON. WHAT STARTS OUT AS A BUSINESS RELATIONSHIP MAY WELL END UP AS A FRIENDSHIP.

"An inner truth about the s..
out to others: Those who are
don't network – they make frie
gain admirers and win trust pre
because their amicable overtures   .o
everyone. A widening circle of influ..ice is
an unintended result, not a calculated one."

Never Eat Alone, Keith Ferrazzi
(Doubleday, 2005)

115

AND NOW ... BACK TO OUR STORY.

I INVITE BILLY TO A ROUND OF GOLF.

116

"Golf was a great idea, Jim. I appreciate the invitation."

"My pleasure, Billy. How is your job search going?"

"Well, as you suggested, I contacted a wider list of people. The best I have is a guy I've met who teaches history at a nearby college."

"Well, that's a start. Do they have a music program at that college?"

"Yes, they do … but no openings."

"Did your buddy say anything about openings in the history department?"

"Oh, OK… well let's talk about that."

"No … but you called him a 'buddy' … I'm not sure our relationship is quite that strong."

119

Billy is not sure what to call the person he knows in the history department. What he's really pondering is the nature of the relationship he has with him. And ultimately about what he might be able to ask of him.

This is our segue to the topic of **social capital**.

120

SOCIAL CAPITAL IS THE STRENGTH OF THE RELATIONSHIP YOU HAVE WITH ANOTHER PERSON.

LIKE ANY OTHER TYPE OF CAPITAL, YOU ONLY HAVE SO MUCH OF IT.

YOU MUST ALWAYS BE THINKING ABOUT EARNING MORE AND, WHEN SPENDING IT, DOING SO PRUDENTLY.

Every relationship you have with another person can be measured in terms of social capital. With very close friends, your supply is almost unlimited. With everyone else, your social capital depends on the length and depth of the relationship you have with that person.

The three glasses of water on the table represent different levels of social capital.

Glass A is the most and that is a close friend. B is second and that is someone you have a nice relationship with. C represents the social capital you have with someone you just met.

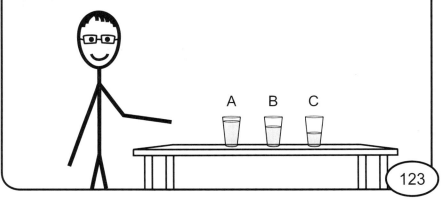

Like water in a glass, social capital can rise and fall.

You can create social capital by building on a relationship.

You can also lose social capital. If, for example, you ask someone you just met for a very big favor – something that a person would feel uncomfortable doing for a new acquaintance – your social capital with that person can decrease.

ASKING FOR TOO MUCH, TOO SOON.

BACK TO BILLY

"What does it matter my relationship with the guy in the history department? I want to teach music."

"Billy, sometimes networking is about connecting the dots. Perhaps your point of entrée into a college music department is to start with an easier transition – the path from high school history teacher to college music instructor may be too steep."

127

"Jim, are you suggesting I apply for a position teaching history at the college?"

"Well, I don't have all the angles figured out. But, I do know that sometimes you need to proceed a step at a time."

128

"But Jim
I'm tired of
teaching
history."

"Hey Billy, I don't make the rules.
You're a history teacher. You
have no experience teaching
music. You have no resume.

If you were the head of a college
music department, would you
hire you?"

129

I won't belabor this point, and it's not just about networking.

While I believe a person should always be seeking new challenges and stretching herself or himself, **realism has to be part of the equation**. Billy could be the world's greatest networker but today he is a long-shot candidate for a role in a college music department.

However, a transition to teaching history in college might position him for a next step into the music department.

130

"I understand your point, Jim, but the fact is I hardly know the history teacher I mentioned. And if there's an opening in the history department, what are you proposing I ask of him?"

"Not sure, Billy. But, let's speak a bit more about social capital."

There is a spectrum of what you can reasonably ask another person to do for you – dependent in part on the social capital you have with that person.

Here are some thoughts as to what Billy might ask his history teacher acquaintance (from low to high):

1. Help Billy understand the hiring process in the history department.

2. Contact Billy if he hears of any openings.

3. Introduce Billy to the people in the department responsible for hiring.

4. Write Billy a recommendation if a position opens up.

5. Make a call to someone on the hiring committee, endorsing Billy for the position.

"Billy, the adept use of social capital is an important part of success. You can't be afraid to ask another person for help, but you also can't push beyond the limits of what's appropriate. This is not an exact science of course.

Why don't you just find out what openings there are or might be in the future, and then let's talk again."

"Yes, good idea."

MY RULES OF SOCIAL CAPITAL

1. Always consider whether your request exceeds the social capital you have with a person.

2. Work at increasing your social capital by building on relationships.

3. Don't presume anything. You may think that what you are asking should be no big deal but, be cautious about that. You don't know the other person's situation.

4. Be careful not to lose social capital. If the nature or frequency of your requests is excessive, you can create ill will.

5. You can never have enough social capital – even more important perhaps than the number of your contacts is the amount of social capital you have within your network.

The point of networking is NOT to have a lot of people who know your name or will take your call. **The point of networking is to have a lot of people WHO WILL TRY TO HELP YOU when you ask.**

Many people confuse knowing someone with actually having a beneficial relationship.

Every person you know has multiple demands on him or her. Every day all of us have to make decisions about the multiple demands on us. When you ask someone for help – no matter what it is – that person has to make a decision among competing demands.

Your goal in networking is to have as many people as possible who will make a decision – among multiple demands – to do what they can do to help you.

"If you know a lot of people but can't get their help, it's a waste of time to keep increasing your number of contacts. On the other hand, if you're highly skilled at getting members of your network to respond to you when you need them, you don't need a huge Rolodex. When both work in conjunction, there's virtually nothing you can't accomplish."

Smart Networking, Liz Lynch
(McGraw Hill, 2009)

MY THINKING ON ASKING ANOTHER'S HELP

I do believe that most people want to help others. It's just that since I never know how my request will affect another, I **don't presume** I have the social capital to ask. Instead I think to myself:

"I'm going to ask this person for something that may be difficult for her to do.

How can I show her that by helping me, she will be helping herself?"

Let me give you an example.

Recently I called a woman I know who is on the Board of Directors of a large company. I asked her to introduce me to the CEO of the company.

I had no insight into whether that request would be a big deal for the woman. Perhaps she was avoiding the CEO for her own reasons and did not want to reach out to him. Who knows? So, I presumed that what I was asking for was a big deal.

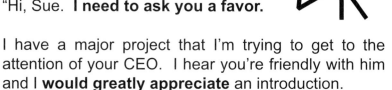

Here is exactly what I said to her:

"Hi, Sue. **I need to ask you a favor.**

I have a major project that I'm trying to get to the attention of your CEO. I hear you're friendly with him and I **would greatly appreciate** an introduction.

However, **I don't want you to do this** if it's uncomfortable for you. **We've helped each other a lot over the years** – and I'm sure **will do so a lot in the future** – so, if this is awkward right now, don't worry about it."

LET'S PARSE MY REQUEST

1. I was direct and to the point.

2. I stated my anticipated appreciation ("would greatly appreciate").

3. I gave her an out – people hate to be pressured.

4. I reminded her that I had been helpful to her in the past.

5. I proposed that I could be helpful to her in the future.

As it turned out, she was happy to help me.

But, by asking in a way that did not **presume** her assistance, I increased the odds of her **wanting** to help and actually doing so in a whole-hearted manner.

OK, I want to make one more point about social capital.

EFFECTIVE NETWORKERS OFTEN HELP PEOPLE WITH NO ASSURANCE OR EVEN EXPECTATION OF PAYBACK.

GREAT NETWORKERS BUILD THEIR SOCIAL CAPITAL OVER A LIFETIME – HELPING WHOEVER THEY CAN.

143

One writer suggests that creating social capital is like throwing a boomerang. You don't know exactly how good things will come back to you, but they do.

144

The networking game is not about investing X with the expectation of immediately earning Y. It is about creating bridges that are there to walk across if and when you need to.

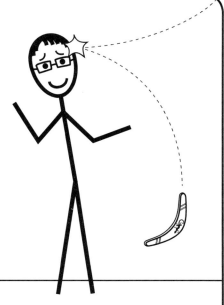

"If you're expecting to find a direct, immediate correlation between your networking activities and the dollars you harvest, you're going to be sorely disappointed. ... The returns you receive through networking are like the apples you pick from an orchard you started from a single seed. (Eventually) that tree will not only bear fruit but also spread the seeds that will ultimately become a whole grove of apple trees."

Networking Like a Pro,
Misner, Alexander & Hilliard
(Entrepreneur Press, 2009)

If you want to be a great networker (and a good person), treat **everyone** you meet with kindness and respect ... not just important types who may be able to do something for you.

First reason is karma. If you send good out into the world, good usually comes back to you.

Second, you never know. There are a lot of powerful people who started their careers in the metaphorical "mail room."

"Thank you, young man. Now if you touch me again, I'm going to call the cops!"

149

A FEW DAYS AFTER OUR GOLF OUTING, I GET A CALL FROM BILLY.

"Jim, I'm going to apply for a position in the history department. It's not my ultimate goal but, if I get hired, it gets me in the door at the college. Perhaps I can then figure out a way to work myself into the music department."

"Sounds good, Billy."

150

SOMETIMES THE PATH FROM WHERE YOU ARE TO WHERE YOU WANT TO BE IS DIRECT.

SOMETIMES IT'S CIRCUITOUS.

EXPLORE ALL AVENUES.

THE BETTER NETWORKED YOU ARE, THE MORE AVENUES YOU HAVE TO EXPLORE.

151

THAT EVENING

152

DINNER AT BETH AND BILLY'S HOUSE

"Jim, Billy has told me so much about you and we do appreciate your help. Would you mind giving us a mini-tutorial about LinkedIn?

"Love to."

LinkedIn is a social network, not unlike Facebook, but used primarily for business purposes. It happens to be the largest, but there are others.

LinkedIn suggests you create a Profile – a description of yourself – and then invite people you know to be your direct connections. When you post information about yourself, your direct connections are notified.

In addition, and this is important, you can learn about the connections of your direct connections.

Let me give you an example.

Suppose Billy has 10 direct connections and one of them is me. Suppose I also have 10 direct connections. By accepting Billy's invitation to be linked to him, I'm allowing him to see the profiles of my connections. Assume that the other 9 of Billy's direct connections also have 10 connections. So, Billy now has 100 new people in his expanded network who may be able to help him.

"I'm still a little confused, Jim."

The top row are Billy's first-tier links or direct connections. Each of them has 10 of their own first-tier links. LinkedIn allows Billy to see the profiles of his direct connections' first-tier contacts.

So, if Billy sees someone in this second tier he thinks might be able to help him, he can go to his first-tier contact and ask for an introduction.

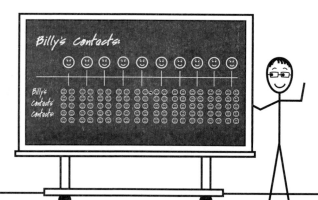

"In this way, Billy expands his network. Although he does not know anyone in his second tier personally, he may be able to reach her through her relationship with his first-tier contact."

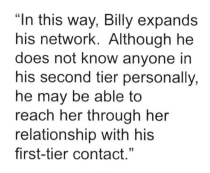

"I think I get it.

Does LinkedIn work?"

"Well, there are several success stories LinkedIn promotes as reasons for joining the network. People who found jobs, investors, customers, and other important business needs by using LinkedIn. In my opinion, it can be a useful tool, among others, for finding and accessing people who may be able to help you."

The point of LinkedIn is to help you expand your network. There are many other ways to do that online.

Here are some:

Sites that connect people of similar interests/locations: **www.netparty.com**

Sites that connect people with similar backgrounds: **www.alumni.cornell.edu**

Sites that connect people with specific needs: **www.domystuff.com**

Sites that connect people with similar philosophies: **www.cure2.com**

SUCCESSFUL NETWORKERS ACCESS ALL RESOURCES – BOTH ONLINE AND OFFLINE – TO REACH THE PEOPLE THEY NEED TO.

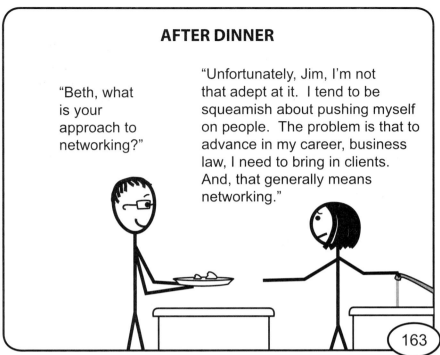

"I'm sure you do ... Beth, there are a lot of ways to network. You don't have to be one of those people constantly promoting herself to others.

On the other hand, if people don't know what you do, they can't seek your services."

"I get that, Jim. But I don't like asking people for anything. When I market myself, when I reach out to people in a business way, I feel like a solicitor. I feel a little icky."

165

"Beth, there are many ways to network yourself without being offensive."

"Any suggestions?"

166

"Gee, Beth, I have suggestions for just about everything.

As my wife says about me, 'sometimes wrong, but never in doubt.'"

"I'm sure your wife is kidding... anyway, I'm interested in any advice you might have."

"Beth, I think the best way to network for business opportunities – in your case to build a following of clients – is to put yourself in non-business situations with people who may one day need your services."

"I have started to get involved in my community, Jim. In fact, I'm a volunteer EMT."

171

"Now, Beth, if you decide to change your specialty to litigation – suing people – working as an EMT might make a lot of sense."

"Jim, I'm no ambulance chaser."

172

"I'm just kidding, Beth.

Since I assume the people who use your services are bankers, brokers and entrepreneurs, perhaps you should join organizations where those people are members."

"That makes sense, and I'll look into organizations to join, but since I'm not the most outgoing person in the world, I was thinking that perhaps I should start writing about my expertise. Perhaps a blog – as a way to market myself."

"Great idea, Beth."

• • • • •

Networking is about extending yourself.

One way to do that is to enhance your visibility by writing and speaking about your expertise. If you become a respected blogger, for example, or develop a following to an e-letter or a column, you "meet" people virtually.

NETWORKING GRAVITY

As people learn about you, they may actually seek you out. One networking expert calls this "network gravity" – processes where people are **drawn toward you** (as contrasted to your reaching out to people).

175

"When I first started my business, I was frustrated by how much time networking took. ... I thought there had to be a better way to use my time and get a bigger bang from my efforts. How could I network smart so that I didn't have to network hard?

I asked myself the same question my management consulting clients ask me ... 'Since we can't focus on everything at once, what's the best way to deploy our limited resources of time, people, and money to reach our goals?'

Rather than focus on just building your network, focus on building your <u>networking gravity</u> *at the same time. Networking gravity is a force that draws people automatically into your world with whom you have the greatest potential to build mutually beneficial relationships."*

Smart Networking,
Liz Lynch (McGraw-Hill, 2009)

176

Here is my list of the kinds of things that can help you develop networking gravity:

1. Write or speak publicly about your expertise.
2. Do great work so that people will talk about you.
3. Tell people about your successes – without being boastful.
4. Study the PR business – seek placements in or interviews from the media.
5. Ask people to recommend prospective customers to you.

NETWORKING GRAVITY IS WHAT HAPPENS WHEN YOU ATTRACT PEOPLE TOWARD YOU. WORKING THE "CROWD" ONE-ON-ONE IS TOUGH. CREATING SITUATIONS WHERE PEOPLE SEEK YOU OUT IS MUCH MORE STRATEGIC.

Sometimes other people will do your networking for you. When you are good at what you do, people will talk about you.

In other words, excellence is in itself a form of networking.

Let me tell you a story about one of my heroes, Vince Lombardi — it helps make my point.

Lombardi is a Hall of Fame football coach, one of the greatest ever.

But, upon graduating college in 1937, he had no idea what he wanted to do. He tried corporate work and even enrolled in law school. But he dropped out of both.

Then one day, a high school football coach asked a friend whether he knew anyone who might be a good assistant coach.

The friend suggested a college teammate of theirs, Lombardi.

"But, I thought he was going into the priesthood," said the high school coach.

"No, he's not doing anything," said the friend.

And so the coach called Lombardi.

The rest is history.

The man who suggested Lombardi had remembered him as a hard-working athlete ... and a real competitor.

And so he recommended Lombardi for the assistant coaching position. In other words, Lombardi's work ethic had inspired others to "network" for him.

I want to make one other point about networking gravity – processes that attract people toward you.

The power of your gravity is dependent upon th**e FREQUENCY** of your messages.

It's not enough to write one article or give a couple of speeches. In order to maximize the power of networking, you have to be omnipresent. If writing or speaking is your thing, then do lots of it. If you are a great "schmoozer," then move around as much as possible.

One of the best networkers I know is a legend in my area. He seems to be everywhere at once.

One Sunday morning a friend of mine told me he had chatted with "the legend" the night before at a hockey game.

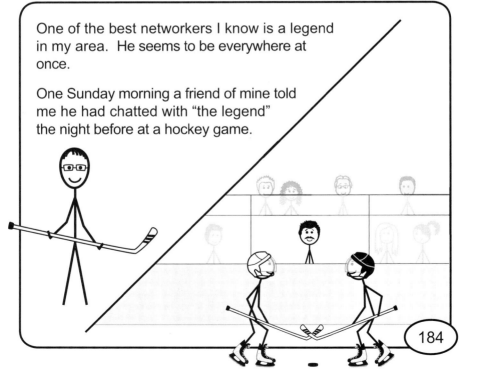

That same Sunday morning another friend told me he had chatted with "the legend" the night before at a basketball game. "Huh?" I said to myself.

So I called "the legend" and asked – "Hey which was it – were you at the hockey game or the basketball game last night?"

"Both. First the hockey game, left after the first period. Had a car take me to basketball game and caught the last quarter. Both big games, Jimbo. Never hurts to be seen where the people are."

As you might guess, "the legend" is a successful business person.

BUT ENOUGH ABOUT THE HYPERACTIVE. LET'S GET BACK TO BETH.

"Wow! That legend guy is a serious networker.

By the way, how was the roast beef?"

"Excellent, Beth … really excellent."

Beth's roast beef was actually a little salty. But, so what? It was nice of her to invite me over.

And, now – like most people – I feel the desire to reciprocate.

INVITATIONS CREATE A SENSE OF RECIPROCITY. WHEN SOMEONE DOES SOMETHING NICE FOR YOU, YOU USUALLY FEEL THE DESIRE TO DO SOMETHING NICE IN RETURN.

CLEVER NETWORKERS ARE VERY ADEPT AT USING INVITATIONS TO BUILD ON RELATIONSHIPS.

FAST FORWARD THIRTY DAYS.

BILLY HAS GOOD NEWS.

"Hey Billy, that's great news! I'm very happy for you… Yes, sure, I can meet you tomorrow.

See you then."

Billy called to tell me that he got a job as an adjunct in the college history department. I'm happy for him. By the way, this book is no fairy tale… Billy was very well qualified for that position **although** his having an acquaintance in the department probably didn't hurt.

I'm a little curious as to why Billy wants to meet with me.

I look forward to seeing him of course but I have a queasy feeling in my stomach.

THE NEXT DAY

"So, Jim, I was thinking about what you said about finding a connector and asking for help when I had a very precise need."

"Yes, I said that, Billy."

"Good, I just wanted to be sure, Jim.

You see I've been poking around the college and found that the music department may be expanding next year. I even got the name of the woman in charge of the expansion. I'm trying to find a way to meet her."

UH OH.

195

"I've tried to contact her myself but she hasn't responded. I'm thinking that if I can just get an introduction to her, she'll meet with me.

You're the most connected person I know, Jim. I was hoping you could help me."

UH OH^2.

196

Billy, has certainly called my bluff. Now it's time for me to put up, or shut up. I told Billy that I believed in helping people. That I'm committed to the proposition that doing good for others – without any specific sense of reciprocity – is the way to be.

197

"I've even done the groundwork for you, Jim. The woman I need to meet is a graduate of New York University. Her maiden name is Sherry Baye. She graduated from NYU at about the same time as your wife, Carol."

"Wow, Billy, I'm impressed. So, are you asking me to ask Carol if she knows a Sherry Baye? And if she does, to make an introduction for you?"

198

"Good news, Billy. Carol does remember Sherry Baye from college. She hasn't had any contact with her in twenty years. But, she has agreed to reach out to her."

"Jim, please be sure to tell Carol how much I appreciate what she is doing. Tell her that although we've never met, she will have a lifelong friend in me. Tell her that I'm available to reciprocate whenever and however I can."

205

So, here's where we are:

Billy needs an introduction to Sherry Baye. Carol went to college with Sherry Baye twenty years ago. Carol feels awkward reaching out to Sherry.

While not exactly a cold call, it's understandable that Carol feels uncomfortable calling or e-mailing Sherry after 20 years.

Let's talk about cold calling.

206

COLD CALLING IS TOUGH. REACHING OUT TO SOMEONE YOU DON'T KNOW (OR HAVEN'T CONNECTED WITH IN A LONG TIME) OR, HAVEN'T BEEN INTRODUCED TO CAN BE DIFFICULT.

BUT, IT'S PART OF BEING A GREAT NETWORKER.

207

I'm shivering for visual effect. Don't you feel a little chilly just looking at me?

The point is, that some people do actually shiver a bit when they have to make a cold call. Cold calls are scary.

208

To carry the metaphor a bit further, to be a great networker, you also have to, at times, be an icebreaker. You occassionally need to initiate relationships and reach out to someone you don't know or don't have an introduction to.

It can be frightening because we all have a primal fear of rejection.

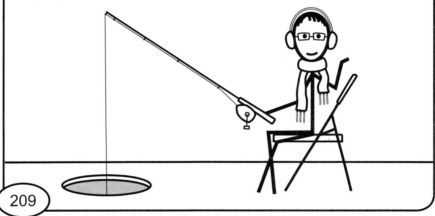

At times I've had to reach out to people I had no connection with, or introduction to. Sometimes the results were positive, sometimes not. But, so what? Nobody has shot me yet. Nobody has screamed at me to get lost.

Reaching out to people you don't know is a bit of an art. I am going to give Carol the ten-point guide I've made for contacting someone cold. Maybe it will help her as she contemplates contacting Sherry Baye.

MY RULES FOR CONTACTING SOMEONE COLD

1. If a call, rehearse. If an e-mail, re-read.
2. E-mail is better than a phone call.
3. Be very direct. Explain the point of the meeting.
4. Suggest how meeting might be mutually beneficial.
5. Reference a commonality (person or place) if you can.
6. Be specific as to how much time you want (as brief as possible).
7. Indicate your flexibility as to when, where and how.
8. If appropriate, flatter ("I've admired your work for years").
9. State your anticipated appreciation.
10. If at first you don't succeed (you get no response), try again.

211

Assuming your cold call was successful and you've gotten a meeting, that first meeting can be critical.

Here's my list of ten rules for that first meeting.

212

1. Be yourself.

2. People aren't that interested in your family.

3. A firm handshake but not a knuckle cruncher.

4. Hold eye contact – not intense glaring however.

5. Listen, listen, listen.

I want to stop here for a moment and speak to the art of listening.

There is no more powerful technique for winning a person over than sincere and attentive listening. In Dale Carnegie's great book, **How to Win Friends and Influence People**, he speaks to the art of listening and relates the words of a man who had met Sigmund Freud:

*"Never had I seen such concentrated attention. There was none of that piercing 'soul penetrating gaze' business. His eyes were mild and genial. His voice was low and kind. His gestures were few. But the attention he gave me, his appreciation of what I said … **You've no idea what it means to be listened to like that**."*

More rules for that first meeting:

6. Convey energy – not arm-waving but quiet strength.

7. Even if you are tired or anxious or hurting, show positivity.

8. Mirror the other person's vocabulary, tempo and body language.

9. Establish the next event/time of contact.

10. Leave on a high point – "great meeting you."

NOW THAT WE'RE MORE COMFORTABLE COLD CALLING, LET'S CHECK BACK WITH CAROL.

"So what do you propose I say to her? 'Hi Sherry, I realize it's been 20 years but remember the time you borrowed my scarf ... Well, you never returned it.'"

217

"Honey, honesty is always the best policy. How about an e-mail?"

Hi Sherry... It's Carol Olson. Hopefully you remember me from NYU – curly red hair, Carmen Hall.

I'm really sorry we lost touch and now after all this time, I'm calling to ask you a favor Ugh..

A friend of my husband would very much like to meet you. He teaches history at the college where you head the music department. He is a decent guy and just wants ten minutes of your time. I hope you'll meet with him.

Thx, and my apologies for this interruption in your life after twenty years! Warmly, Carol.

218

"Yes, that sounds sensible – until I think about what a jerk Sherry will think I am … why can't you find a real job, like a plumber or a politician?"

"Oh, sweetheart, you're such a kidder. I have a real job… I'm a guide. A teacher. A spokesperson for self-improvement."

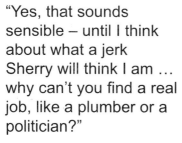

219

"No. No, what you are is a meddler and a a nudge."

220

I do understand Carol's point of view, of course.

But, Billy has asked for help and I've told him that good networkers believe in helping people.

221

FINALLY CAROL GETS UP HER NERVE AND SENDS AN E-MAIL TO SHERRY BAYE.

FORTUNATELY, IT'S VERY WELL RECEIVED.

222

Sherry Baye was very just busy when Billy initially tried to contact her. So, she never responded to his e-mails. But things had eased when she heard from Carol.

Sherry recalled Carol with fond memories. In fact, she remembered that she never returned Carol's scarf.

Although Sherry would have eventually met with Billy in any event, Carol's e-mail got through to her at just the right time. Carol and Sherry are now talking again and plan to have coffee in a few weeks.

And Billy got his audience with Sherry.

BILLY IS VERY GRATEFUL FOR CAROL'S INTERVENTION.

HE INVITES JIM AND CAROL OUT TO DINNER AT A LOCAL RESTAURANT.

"Carol, I really appreciate your getting me in the door with Sherry Baye."

"You're welcome, Billy."

"She is really a lovely woman. We met for 15 minutes and she explained to me what is going on in the music department. In about six months, there may be an entry-level position there for which I will be considered. I could not be happier!"

"And how about you, Beth … how is your networking going?"

"Well, Jim, as you suggested, I've started putting myself into environments with people who need legal services.

Not a lot of payback quite yet but I do see how this approach will have benefits."

"Anything I can do to help?"

227

"Not unless you know someone in the New York Professional Women's Board. It's quite a prestigious organization but you need to know someone to get in."

"The Professional Women's Board …"

228

Don't worry, Carol was not angry at me …
for long. And she was happy to introduce
Beth to her third cousin, a member of the
Professional Women's Board.

It's nice the way things worked out:

1. Through a little help from Sherry Baye and given that
    he was already teaching at the college, Billy was able
    to get a minor position in the music department. He is
    still teaching history, but he now has an opportunity to
    expand his role in the music department.

2. Beth got into the New York Professional Women's
    Board with help from Carol's third cousin. That and
    other networking efforts have helped her increase her
    client base.

3. Carol got a promise from me that I
    will not interfere in people's lives
    for thirty days.

I hope you enjoyed our story. Of course, Billy's and Beth's efforts were just metaphors for whatever it is that YOU want to achieve. Their stories were just to give you ideas. Your own path may be very different, but networking strategies remain constant whatever you seek.

233

Thanks for your time … as with all of our books, I'd like to summarize my views with a top ten list of points you need to remember about networking.

234

#1: MAKE NETWORKING AN IMPORTANT PART OF YOUR BUSINESS STRATEGY.

Many successful people attribute their achievements to the number and diversity of people in their network.

And yet most of us network only when it is convenient. The better approach is to make networking a part of your every-day agenda. Some experts recommend that you spend at least 5 – 10 hours a week networking.

#2: WHEN YOU HAVE A SPECIFIC NEED, START WITH FRIENDS AND FAMILY.

Although you may think you're already aware of who your closest friends and family members know, don't assume anything.

Remember Bob Beaudine's theory – you may already know someone who knows the person you are trying to reach.

#3: WHEN YOU WANT SOMETHING, BE PRECISE IN EXPLAINING IT TO OTHERS.

If you do not explain with clarity and precision exactly what you are trying to accomplish, people won't be able to help you.

#4: REACH OUTSIDE YOUR COMFORT ZONE.

The power of your network is measured not only by the number of people in it but also by the diversity of the people in it.

If you don't go outside your comfort zone in extending yourself to people, and being receptive to overtures to you, you risk creating a network that is filled with people just like you. This is much less powerful than a web of people who have different contacts, philosophies, professions and backgrounds.

#5: FIND CONNECTORS AND BUDDY UP TO THEM.

Connectors (think Steve Siegel) know lots and lots of people. If they like and trust you, they will be powerful resources when you need help reaching someone. And connectors know other connectors. So, by identifying and affiliating with modern-day Paul Revere's, you increase the likelihood of finding someone who can help you.

#6: THE INTERNET CAN BE A SUPER-POWERFUL CONNECTOR.

Sites like Facebook and LinkedIn perform some of the same functions as a connector.

On those sites, you can reach many more people than you actually know.

#7: DON'T ASSUME PEOPLE WILL HELP YOU JUST TO BE NICE. GIVE THEM A REASON TO HELP YOU.

There are some people in your life who will help you no matter what. Others need a reason to help you … and that reason is almost always an answer to the question "What's in it for me?"

If you want to get the most out of other people, show them that you understand the principle of reciprocity, and that helping you will one day come back to them in spades.

#8: GIVE BEFORE YOU RECEIVE.

Great networkers understand that a broad and powerful network is built over time.

Create your network in advance of when you need help. By giving without keeping score, you establish relationships. And, when you need something, those relationships will be great resources.

#9: BE AWARE OF YOUR SOCIAL CAPITAL.

When you need help from another person, consider what social capital you have with him or her. Don't push it. Social capital is built up gradually. If you attempt to make a withdrawal before you have enough social capital, you may harm your relationship.

#10: DON'T SEE NETWORKING AS JUST ABOUT BUSINESS.

Networking is about meeting and getting to know others. Although it is a powerful business strategy – maybe the most powerful – it is also a wonderful way to grow as a person.

By reaching out to people – and by being receptive to people who reach out to you – you open your horizons to new friendships and personal growth.

THE END.

CONCLUSION

We here at **The Skinny On**™ hope you enjoyed this book. We would love to hear your comments.

My personal e-mail is jrandel@randmediaco.com.

Warm regards,

Jim Randel

Here is a list of some of the books we reviewed in preparing *The Skinny on Networking*:

15 Secrets Every Network Marketer Must Know, Rubino and Terhune (Wiley, 2006)

Achieving Success Through Social Capital, Wayne Baker (Josey-Bass, 2000)

Breakthrough Networking, Lillian Bjorseth (Duoforce, 2009)

Dig Your Well Before You're Thirsty, Harvey Mackay (Doubleday, 1997)

Getting A Job, Mark Granovetter (University of Chicago Press, 1974)

Highly Effective Networking, Orville Pierson (Career Press, 2009)

How to Win Friends and Influence People, Dale Carnegie (Simon and Schuster, 1936)

Life is a Contact Sport, Ken Kragen (William Morrow, 1994)

Linchpin, Seth Godin (Penguin, 2010)

Little Black Book of Connections, Jeffrey Gitomer (Bard Press, 2006)

Make Your Contacts Count, Baber and Waymon (AMACOM, 2007)

Masters of Networking, Misner and Morgan (Bard Press, 2000)

Me 2.0: Build a Power Brand to Archive Career Success, Dan Schwabel (Kaplan, 2009)

Networking Like a Pro, Misner, Alexander and Hilliard (Entrepreneur Press, 2009)

Never Eat Alone, Keith Ferrazzi (Doubleday, 2005)

Power Networking, Fisher and Vilas (Bard Press, 2000)

Professional Networking for Dummies, Donna Fisher (Wiley, 2001)

Smart Networking, Liz Lynch (McGraw Hill, 2009)

The 29% Solution, Misner and Donovan (Greenleaf, 2008)

The Power of Small, Thaler and Koval (Broadway Books, 2009)

The Power of Who, Bob Beaudine (Center Street, 2009)

The Tipping Point, Malcolm Gladwell (Little Brown, 2000)

Think and Grow Rich, Napoleon Hill (Fawcett, 1937)

Tribes, Seth Godin (Portfolio, 2008)

Whale Done: The Power of Positive Relationships, Ken Blanchard (Free Press, 2002)

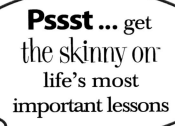

Pssst ... get
the skinny on
life's most
important lessons

Join **The Skinny On**™
community today!

- Get 20% off your first
  purchase

- Receive exclusive offers,
  previews and discounts

- See excerpts from all
  The Skinny On™ books

- Suggest topics for
  new books

- View and subscribe to
  The Skinny On™
  weekly webcomic

- Become a writer for
  The Skinny On™

www.TheSkinnyOn.com

Connect with us on: